My Candid Words

A collection of poems

Chelsea Haye

ISBN-13: 978-1-7352990-1-3 (Hardback)
ISBN-13: 978-1-7352990-0-6 (Paperback)
ISBN-13: 970-1-7352990-2-0 (E-Book)
Library of Congress Control Number: 2020905473

Any references to historical events, real people, or real places are used fictitiously. Names, characters, and places are products of the author's imagination.

Front cover image by Chelsea Haye
Book design by Chelsea Haye

Printed by Amazon.com, Inc., in the United States of America.

www.chelseahaye.com

DEDICATION

I'd like to dedicate this book to the little black boys and girls, who are doing the damn thing. I'd also like to dedicate this to a younger me, already aware of the burden of society.

CONTENTS

Chelsea Haye

Preface

I wrote this book for many reasons. I have been an activist for as long as I can remember. However, I have had trouble finding the best way for me to share my views and ideas. A way in which I can help talk about bigotry and hate. I found that writing is a great way to do it. Leaving hidden messages or being explicit with what you are trying to teach or expose. It has always fascinated me how some of our worlds' greatest writers talk about important issues. This book covers several different important topics. Racism, Climate Change, Police Brutality, Women's Health Reform, etc. Throughout the journey of writing this book, I learned a tremendous amount. Seeing and hearing the different views on each of these topics helped to enrich my own views. I hope to continue on this path wherever it may lead me. Learning is one of the best gifts in life.

To begin with these poems I have to go through a research process. My process changes depending on the topic. A common theme is having to be uncomfortable. You must listen and hear opposing views. It's an extreme advantage to have an idea of the other side's views. Trying to immerse yourself as much as you can is also a part of the process. Relying on anecdotes and real-life stories holds the same value as articles and graphs. Engaging in discussions and arguments helped me to look at flaws in my beliefs and ideas. My recommendation is to start by googling. You won't know what will happen until you take your first steps.

I have many people to thank for the production of this book. I would first like to thank my parents, Marian and Adrian Haye. These two have been instrumental in pushing me to meet deadlines. They have helped me look over my work and make edits. My mother was the first to encourage me to make more poems after a simple writing exercise at school. I found from there I also enjoyed writing detailed stories filled with adventure and fun characters. I would also like to thank my friends who continuously support me. Shout out to Izzy. From supporting my writing to my business. I appreciate you all for pushing me forward.

Chelsea Haye

Two Black Men

By: Chelsea Haye

Two Black Men

sat in a Starbucks.

No crime but their own skin.

We all yell black power,

the police say all matter,

but no one is making any change

Back and Forth

Back and Forth

the politicians go.

Protests and walkouts,

but Trump's not blinking an eye.

He's Proud of his Boys.

I say let it end.

Our lives are not your toys.

To be played with like policies and bills.

I want everybody to think

...think before you do

Let Mothers Tears
By: Chelsea Haye

Let Mothers tears dry.

Black people should die of old age.

Not with bullet holes.

Black Lives Do Matter
By: Chelsea Haye

Black Lives Do Matter.

We have said many times.

All Lives Matter? Please don't undermine.

I said, Black Lives Matter. Don't waste my time.

Will You Listen
By: Chelsea Haye

Will you listen to the cries?

The younger generation rising up.

The politicians don't want no ties.

We will continue to fight, we won't give up.

The same children you avoid

will one day take your place.

So many of us are unemployed.

We know this death is not a faze.

One voice may cause a simple change.

But many could cause a ripple.

Let us stand as a brigade.

Don't think you can belittle,

so many races and genders.

We've only fanned the embers.

We are the Future
By: Chelsea Haye

They say we are the future,

but our futures are being taken away.

The Constitution says "we the people,"

not "we the privileged whites."

Slavery took 346 years.

Jim Crow about 70.

400 odd years since then,

and we still got Racism.

It's never going to end.

We had Barack Obama,

then Donald Trump.

Another racist white man.

That was payback for black.

Other countries are laughing at us.

We care more for the weapon,

than the victims.

Gun debates are going nowhere,

so lives just disappear.

Does the Constitution apply here?

It did back then.

Gun toting citizens believe in,

"the right to bear arms."

We believe in,

"the right to life, liberty, and the pursuit of happiness."

The people have the right to petition.

The government still doesn't listen.

Fight after fight.

The end is glistening.

Racist, Too
By: Chelsea Haye

White people can be racists,

don't say black people too.

It takes years of oppression.

Not one or two.

People are always being oppressed.

The methods have changed,

but yet the missions the same.

It takes hold in each of us.

Unfair
By: Chelsea Haye

It's Unfair.

That I'm one of two,

who struggled to private school.

Don't have the time to play a fool.

My black life comes with a different set of rules.

It's Unfair

Even if I was rich,

life would not go on without a stitch.

Every flinch could be a gun.

Any blink and I must run.

Is killing black lives so fun?

It's not fair.

It's not fair,

that they wake up without a hurry.

Today might be his last. I have to worry.

Will my father get to see his kin?

Or be killed for the color of his skin?

So Unfair

Will I be good enough?

Will I ace that college admission?

Can I afford to pay tuition?

Is it out of my own hands?

It's Unfair.

Hear my anger and my fury.

Fighting for a chance.

Going through life's dance.

It's Unfair.

But I won't give up.

In God I trust.

I'll see the redeeming light.

I won't go out without a fight.

Take a Moment
By: Chelsea Haye

My head hurts.

My feet ache.

My knees are scraped.

I take a moment to listen.

My side itches.

Fingers twitching.

Eyes blinking.

Can't focus.

And I'm hoping you don't notice.

Mind running 99 miles,

and my head hurts.

Side burning.

Fingers cracking.

The sounds that my body procreate.

Can't handle all this debate.

So,

I take a moment.

My Body
By: Chelsea Haye

My Body.

Is it mine?

This body.

Why do you tax it?

This body no longer feels like mine?

Her Body.

Why do you stare at it?

That Body.

She feels she should cover up,

but you claim its your body.

His Body.

Who is he?

It doesn't matter.

A pair of abs and a pretty face.

He is nothing besides a body.

Our Body.

Don't touch it.

Don't look it.

My Body.

His Body.

Her Body.

Their Body.

That's not the only part of me.

In the Kitchen
By: Chelsea Haye

In the Kitchen.

Spices and Sugar mix.

They make colors just like my skin.

Traditions & Culture,

inhabit the stovetop.

Memories kept alive.

Granite counters

and metal stovetops.

Lunch and Dinner.

Fruitful Meals.

Food for the soul

is made here.

In the Kitchen,

I watch Momma.

In the Kitchen,

I watch Poppa.

In the Kitchen,

I watch Grandma.

Making me soul food to eat.

Groans & Sighs
By: Chelsea Haye

When the morning comes,

I hope for something better.

I sigh and groan in anticipation.

I could really use it.

When the night comes,

I sigh in disappointment.

I groan in dissatisfaction.

I don't notice what's around me.

I know that it gets rough.

Doesn't make it any less tough.

My shoulders slump.

My back caves in.

My head lowers from the weight.

My eyes droop.

My nose runs.

My smile disappears from the hate.

Through all the groans and sighs.

I express my disappointment.

At a system never designed for me.

Sirens
By: Chelsea Haye

There sirens won't stop.

Every beat a body drops.

COVIDs got its hands around my neck.

Every cough I hear, every move I sweat.

Every scream sounds near.

All the voices so clear.

News won't turn off no matter how I try.

How can I decipher whats truth and who lies?

Please lord, I don't want to die.

Untitled Poem
By: Chelsea Haye

You have the right to remain silent.

Everything and anything you say or do,

gives me the right to kill you.

You have the right to be persecuted based on your skin.

The same will happen to your children.

You have the right to fear for your life,

day in and day out.

You have the right.

You don't have the right to breathe.

You don't have the right to walk.

You don't have the right to play with a toy.

You don't have the right to reach for a license.

You don't have the right to be in your car.

You don't have the right to walk with your grandfather.

You don't have the right to ask for help.

You don't have the right to be a lawful gun owner.

You don't have the right to sleep at home.

You don't have a right to live in this country.

You don't have a right.

We have the right to protest

We have the right to fight

We have the right to believe

in a future so so bright

We have the right.

Chelsea Haye

ABOUT THE AUTHOR

New-York based, Chelsea Haye, is a high-school student at Brooklyn Friends School. Chelsea has been writing and cultivating her poems for years. This book stands as her first breakthrough into the written world. She enjoys drinking tea and writing adventures for her many characters. She is an older sister and daughter. Chelsea's family holds great importance in her life, encouraging her to write. Writing is a release for Chelsea, you can expect to see and feel her emotions through her words. Her upcoming book, Defective will entail the story of two troubled teenagers and their path to a healthier life. Chelsea's goal is to spread joy and knowledge through her writing. You can visit her and hear about book updates here: https://instagram.com/chelseahaye.

www.ingramcontent.com/pod-product-compliance
Lightning Source LLC
Chambersburg PA
CBHW081242090426
42738CB00016B/3382